Small and Large

By Arlene Block

CELEBRATION PRESS

Pearson Learning Group

Contents

Animals are many sizes.
The same kind of animal
can be different sizes.

Frogs

green mantella

This kind of frog is small.

bullfrog

This kind of frog is large.

Bats

pipistrelle bat

This kind of bat is small.

flying fox bat

This kind of bat is large.

Dogs

Chihuahua

This kind of dog is small.

Great Dane

This kind of dog is large.

Penguins

fairy penguin

This kind of penguin is small.

king penguins

This kind of penguin is large.

Sharks

bamboo shark

This kind of shark is small.

whale shark

This kind of shark is large.

Horses

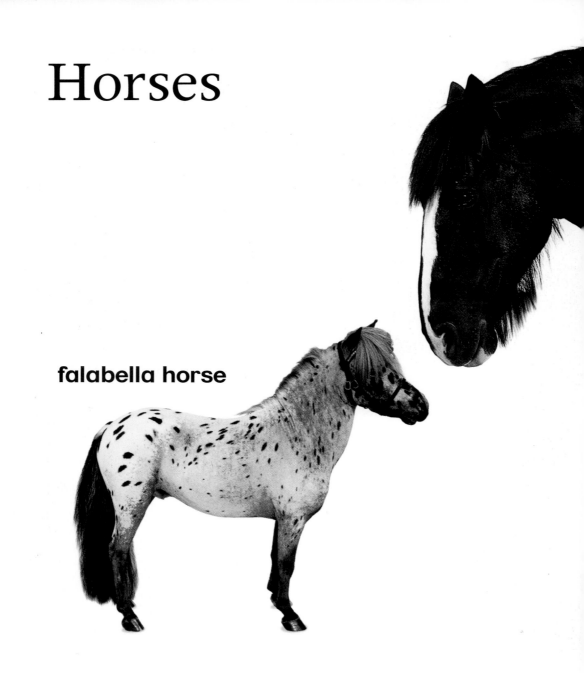

falabella horse

This kind of horse is small.

draft horse

This kind of horse is large.

Animals are many sizes.